The Blueprint to Becoming a Designer

Dana Darr

The Blueprint to Becoming a Designer

ISBN: 9798884637917

DEDICATION

This handbook is dedicated to my father, Dana W. Darr, who passed away in April 2023. He would kick my ass if I settled for being average, and I want this to be your encouragement as a reader to kick yourself to go out there and achieve your dreams. We all must start somewhere in our journey.

The Blueprint to Becoming a Designer

CONTENTS

	Preface	1
1	The Journey Begins	2
2	Starting Your Blueprint	4
3	What The Heck Is UX, UI, & Product Design?	7
4	Envisioning Your Desired Design Role	11
5	When Do You Want to Be There?	14
6	Taking The Initial Steps	16
7	Exploring Niche & Brand	19
8	Paths to Mastery	22
9	Design Tools	24
10	Don't Wait, Start Networking	27
11	Creating a Portfolio	29
12	Creating a Case Study	32
13	Utilize Your Network to Find Volunteer Work	35
14	Building Your Brand	37
15	Be Brave, Show Off Your Work	39
16	Appling for Jobs	42
17	The Long Haul	45
18	Wrapping Up	49
	References	52

PREFACE

This book is dedicated to new designers looking for a guide to start their design career journey. If you feel lost along the way, remember you aren't alone. We have a robust community of designers. I'm available if you ever want more in-depth help in specific subjects. This handbook only scratches the surface of the profound world of design.

A bit about me, the sap writing this thing. I'm originally from Washington State and decided to move to Arizona during COVID. After waking up and hating my job daily, I decided to change. Luckily, I had a powerful friend who has been a fantastic influence throughout my career to propel me. With no formal college degree, I persisted and grinded my way into a new job during one of the most challenging times to get into a field flooded with newbies and recently laid-off designers. Constantly trying new things and figuring them out as I go, I felt many people with similar stories must be out there.

I would love to hear feedback from anyone who reads this handy handbook so that I can improve and know how I can be of better service. I want to help others who are struggling or who have less to find a footing in their career journey.

THE JOURNEY BEGINS

Welcome to "Blueprint to Becoming a Designer," the spirit guide that will equip you with the knowledge and skills to embark on a fulfilling UX, UI, or product designer career. In this book, we will explore the roadmap to success in design, discuss some tips, and empower aspiring designers. Whether you are a self-taught designer, a career switcher, or someone who wants to learn more about the industry, this book will guide you through the steps to kickstart your design career.

Many believe a prestigious college degree is the only way to enter the design industry. However, this book aims to challenge that notion. While formal education can provide a solid foundation, there are other determinants of success. Passion, dedication, and a growth mindset can take you far in this field.

In the coming chapters, we'll embark on self-discovery and career transformation. Understanding yourself, your unique personality traits, and your past career experiences is crucial in shaping your future in design. We'll explore how to weave your narrative and past experiences into a compelling story that adds depth and authenticity to your design career. Whether you're a meticulous planner, a creative thinker, or a problem-solving genius, these traits can be powerful tools in the design world.

We will then explore the various roles within the design industry, from UX and UI designers to product managers and graphic artists. Each role has unique skills and responsibilities; understanding these differences is critical to finding your niche. By highlighting the nuances of each role, you can align your strengths and interests with the right career path in design.

Goal setting is another critical aspect we'll cover. It's about setting lofty ambitions and crafting achievable, step-by-step objectives leading to your ultimate career aspirations. We'll discuss strategies to set realistic goals, how to break them down into manageable tasks, and ways to track your progress.

As we progress, you'll learn where to start when transitioning into your new career. The starting point of reference includes practical advice on building a robust portfolio, networking strategies, and essential tools every designer should know. We'll also delve into the nuances of job hunting in the design world, from crafting a resume that stands out to acing design interviews.

Throughout this book, you'll find various tips and insights that will guide you at the beginning of your journey and support you as you advance in your career. Whether it's staying updated with the latest design trends, continuous learning, or finding a mentor, these nuggets of wisdom will be your companions all the way to the pinnacle of your design career.

Buckle up! The next chapter will explore how to start your career blueprint. You can chart a clear path toward your dream career by defining your goals, identifying your strengths, and understanding the various design disciplines. We will explore the different areas of design, the skills required, and the opportunities available, helping you make informed decisions about your future.

As you take off on this journey toward becoming a designer, remember that success is not measured solely by your academic background but by your passion, perseverance, and willingness to learn. Start thinking about what drives you to begin a journey toward success.

STARTING YOUR BLUEPRINT

This chapter will dig into the essential aspects of becoming a designer. We will explore the connection between your identity and the world of design, understand the importance of your background, and discuss the skills you have built throughout your life. Furthermore, we will discover how you can utilize these skills to propel your career as a designer. Pull out a pen and paper to begin writing as we read this chapter. Now is as good a time as any to brush up on your notetaking skills!

Your Identity and Design

Design is an inherently personal and subjective discipline. It thrives on the unique perspectives, experiences, and talents each individual brings to the table. Understanding who you are and how that relates to design is crucial for starting your growth as a designer.

Reflect on your interests, values, and passions that have shaped you thus far. It helps to think about what or who introduced you to this creative career, the root of where inspiration hit you in the face. If you aren't lucky enough to be hit in the face, then ask your closest friends and family. Identify the areas that ignite your creativity and fuel your motivation. Embrace these elements as they will shape your design journey and contribute to your distinctive style.

Go back further in your professional history and think about where you started. Maybe you came from years of customer service work - that can be an asset. Learning to communicate and meld with different personalities may make you adept at understanding users or cross-communication between teams in your new company. Learn to think of everything you have done in your past as an asset and not a hindrance. You may be surprised by what you can translate into this new career.

Consider your personality traits and how they align with the different aspects of design. Are you analytical, detail-oriented, or imaginative? Recognize your strengths and keep digging to leverage them in your design practice. Embracing your unique traits and weaknesses will help you find a proper fit when you pick the design area you want to stick to.

Exploring Your Background

Your background, including your cultural heritage, educational experiences, and personal history, significantly shapes your design perspective. Recognizing and embracing these influences is essential to fostering a deeper understanding of yourself and the design realm.

Reflect on your educational journey and how it has contributed to your design skills. Whether you pursued formal design education or learned through self-study and practical experience, acknowledge the knowledge and insights gained from your education. These experiences have equipped you with a foundation to build upon.

Sidenote for all who are self-learners: the beautiful thing about technology is that there are a million different resources. You need to know where to look and what form of learning suits you best.

Developing Your Skill Set

Design requires a diverse skill set that encompasses technical abilities and creative thinking. Now that you have a list of traits and skills that portray who you are, it's time to start throwing spaghetti at the wall and see what sticks. You do have that pen and paper we spoke about earlier.

If you have no prior knowledge of design, don't worry! There are still ways to apply the skills and traits you have identified from your background. First, start by immersing yourself in the world of design. Whether that is UX, UI, or product design, it doesn't matter. Read books, watch tutorials, and explore online resources to familiarize yourself with design principles, techniques, and tools. Many people start with a simple Google search, but we suggest you go with how you learn best. For example, if it's by reading, then read. If it's by doing, sign up for some courses and do. You get the picture!

Here is a link to my free resources!
danadarr.info

Additionally, consider seeking guidance from mentors or enrolling in design courses to gain practical knowledge and hands-on experience. Take advantage of opportunities to collaborate with experienced designers or participate in design competitions to enhance your skills further. An example of a design competition is a Hack-a-thon. You can find some that require designers rather than just developers.

Remember, design is a field that values diverse perspectives and backgrounds. By leveraging your identified skills and traits, even without prior design knowledge, you can bring a unique and valuable perspective to the table and significantly impact the design world.

Utilizing Your Skill Set

Having built a repertoire of skills and some ideas of how they can be applied, it is essential to understand how to employ them to advance your career as a designer effectively. As you go along, you will begin to identify what type of designer you resonate with the most.

Identify the design field or specialization that aligns with your skills and interests. An example of a specialization may be writing, creating pretty color palettes, and typography for branding. The possibilities are endless. By focusing on a specific niche, you can hone your expertise and establish yourself as an authority in that area, opening opportunities for growth and recognition. Many job descriptions will demand many skills upfront, but a designer can only be so good at all these things. It's desirable to be the best at what you love and passable at other side skills versus being subpar at ten different random skills that a company may demand.

Collaborating and Networking

Leverage your skills to collaborate with other designers, creatives, and professionals. Actively engage in design communities, attend events, and build a strong network. Collaborative projects and connections can lead to new opportunities, exposure to different perspectives, and a chance to learn from others. Networking will be ingrained into your soul by the end of this book. It's essential; you will hear that others believe the same.

To stay relevant in the ever-evolving design industry, staying updated with the latest trends and technologies is crucial. By staying ahead of the curve, you can continue to grow and adapt as a designer, ensuring your work remains fresh. Keep your eyes peeled to see what new updates Figma, a popular design tool, may have. Find great YouTube channels to follow if you prefer to max out your screen time. Whatever it takes, there is no shame in the game because this is about you.

Remember, becoming a successful designer is a continuous process of learning, exploring, and refining your skills. Embrace the challenges, seek out new opportunities, and never stop pushing. If this is enjoyable, the immense task of "continuous learning" may not be too bad.

Understanding who you are as a designer and utilizing the skills you have built are integral steps to becoming a successful designer. This whole chapter was about learning who you are, finding learning resources, and seeing what area of design you are starting to match with. We will investigate the differences between UX, UI, and product designers.

WHAT THE HECK IS UX, UI, AND PRODUCT DESIGN?

"Design is not just what it looks like and feels like. Design is how it works." - Steve Jobs.

In the Wild West of design, various specializations cater to different aspects of creating exceptional user experiences. This chapter aims to explore the three prominent areas of design: User Experience (UX) design, User Interface (UI) design, and (Digital) Product Design. We will investigate each field's definitions, required skills, career roles, and salary averages. Understanding the distinctions between these design disciplines is crucial for aspiring designers to carve out their path in the industry.

Understanding UX Design

UX (User Experience) design is the art and science of creating optimal user experiences by understanding and catering to their needs, behaviors, and emotions. This field goes beyond aesthetics, crafting a seamless journey from the user's first interaction with a product to the final goal. A UX designer aims to forge intuitive, user-centric interfaces that amplify usability and enhance user satisfaction. If you're fascinated by the psychology of users and passionate about designing solutions that resonate with their needs, UX design offers a fulfilling and challenging path.

UX design demands a unique mix of analytical thinking, empathy, and creativity. A proficient UX designer must have a strong foundation in user research techniques, enabling them to uncover deep insights into user needs and behaviors. Skills in information architecture are crucial for organizing and structuring content logically and navigably for users.

A UX designer should also be adept at creating wireframes and prototypes, essential for visualizing and testing design concepts. Usability testing skills are vital to ensure the end product is user-friendly and meets the intended goals. Additionally, strong communication and collaborative abilities are imperative for working effectively with cross-functional teams, including UI designers, developers, and product managers, and articulating design ideas and user insights to stakeholders.

UX designers are central figures in multidisciplinary teams, often bridging the gap between users and the technical team. Their role encompasses conducting thorough user research, developing user personas, and mapping user flows. These foundational activities inform the creation of wireframes and prototypes, which are then iteratively refined through usability testing.

This process ensures that the final product aligns closely with user expectations and needs, thus enhancing the overall user experience. By focusing on the user, UX designers play a critical role in ensuring that products are functional but also enjoyable and accessible.

Salaries for UX designers can vary significantly based on factors like experience, geographic location, and industry sector. Based on recent sources, the average salary for a UX Designer in the U.S. is around $78,417 per year (*UX Designer Salary in 2023 | PayScale*, n.d.). For example, in high-paying cities like San Francisco, the average can go up to $129,655 (*2023 UX Designer Salary in US | Built In*, n.d.).

Additionally, Salary.com reports that the average base salary for a UX Designer ranges from $91,361 to $120,319, with the average being $104,613 (Salary.com, n.d.). This range suggests a significant variation based on experience level, specific skills, and the company's size.

In summary, UX design is a dynamic and impactful field requiring diverse skills and a deep understanding of user needs. It offers a rewarding career path for those passionate about improving users' interactions with digital products and services.

Understanding UI Design

UI (User Interface) design is the creative and technical process of designing the interfaces through which users interact with digital products and services. This field focuses on the visual aspects of the user experience, including screen layout, interactive elements, typography, color schemes, and overall visual communication. UI design is more than just visually appealing designs; it's about ensuring that interfaces are intuitive and accessible and facilitating a seamless interaction between the user and the product. If you are passionate about visual storytelling and crafting interfaces that connect with users, UI design offers an exciting and rewarding career path.

A successful UI designer must have a sharp eye for aesthetics and a solid grasp of design principles. Proficiency in visual design tools such as Adobe Photoshop, Sketch, or Figma is crucial. Understanding typography, color theory, and responsive design principles is critical to creating visually compelling and cohesive interfaces. A UI designer's toolkit also includes skills in developing and applying design systems and understanding different platforms and devices' technical constraints and possibilities.

UI designers are crucial in translating the UX design into a visually engaging and interactive interface. They work closely with UX designers, developers, and stakeholders to ensure the visual design aligns with the overall user experience strategy. Their role involves creating style guides, designing pixel-perfect interfaces, and ensuring that the visual aspects of the product are consistent across different platforms.

The salary for UI designers varies based on experience, location, and industry. In 2023, the average salary for a UI Designer in the U.S. was approximately $84,837, with a typical salary range being between $90,000 and $100,000 (2023 UI Designer Salary in US | Built In, n.d.) (User Interface Designer Salary in 2023 | PayScale, n.d.). However, this can vary, with PayScale reporting an average base salary of $71,005 (User Interface Designer Salary in 2023 | PayScale, n.d.-b) and Salary.com noting a range between $90,588 and $109,740 (Salary.com, n.d.-a). Senior UI designers with more experience can expect higher salaries, often above $100,000 annually.

Understanding Product Design

Product design in the digital realm is an end-to-end process that encompasses creating digital products from the initial idea to the final execution. This multifaceted discipline blends UX (User Experience) and UI (User Interface) design elements to develop cohesive user experiences across various touchpoints. A product design career could be perfect if you are pulled into owning a product's life cycle. It requires a holistic approach where both form and function are considered to ensure the product looks appealing and efficiently meets users' needs.

A successful product designer possesses a diverse skill set that includes but is not limited to, UX research, interaction design, visual design, prototyping, and effective collaboration. It's crucial to deeply understand user needs and business objectives to create user-centric products while aligning with the product's overall strategy. This role involves a balance of technical skills, creative flair, and the ability to see the bigger picture and how each design decision impacts the user experience and business goals.

Product designers work closely with cross-functional teams, including UX/UI designers, developers, product managers, and marketers. Their responsibilities encompass defining product goals, conducting user research, and creating wireframes and prototypes. They also play a significant role in the visual design of interfaces, ensuring that the product's implementation aligns with its design intention.

The salary for product designers varies widely, depending on factors such as experience, location, and the industry they work in. As of 2023, the average salary for a Product Designer in the U.S. is approximately $90,439, typically between $60,000 and $135,000 (Salary.com, n.d.-a). Built In also reports an average salary of $112,119 for product designers (2023 Product Designer Salary in US | Built In, n.d.). In contrast, Salary.com suggests a lower range, with average base salaries between $58,807 and $73,637 (Salary.com, n.d.-a). These variations highlight the importance of considering specific job roles, locations, and industries when evaluating potential earnings in product design.

The Job Market

The tech job market has been bumpy through 2023. Across all three disciplines, a common theme is the need to adapt and evolve with technological advancements and changing user expectations. Designers who continue to learn, expand their skill set, and embrace new technologies will be well-positioned in the job market in 2024 and beyond. Standing out in any way you can manage will go far.

Understanding the differences between UX, UI, and product design is crucial for aspiring designers. While UX design focuses on creating meaningful user experiences, UI design emphasizes visually appealing interfaces, and Product Design combines both disciplines to create seamless digital products. Each field requires a unique skill set and offers various career opportunities. In the next chapter, we will explore how to envision your desired design role and set goals to achieve career success!

ENVISIONING YOUR DESIGN ROLE

Where do you want to be? Envision your end goal in your career hunt as a designer. Having a clear vision of where you want to be is essential to set a direction for your career. Remember not to place yourself inside of a box. Go outside of the box and set your goals high. This goal has no time limit, so take the reach and see what's out there. This chapter will explore different aspects to consider when envisioning your desired goals!

Work Styles

One of the first things to think about is the work environment. Consider your working style and personal preferences to determine what environment suits you best. Do you prefer the flexibility of working remotely, the balance of a hybrid setup, or the collaborative atmosphere of an office? Be honest and know that sometimes you must try one to see if you love or hate it.

Another decision is whether you want to work as a freelance designer or a full-time company employee. Freelancing offers flexibility and the opportunity to work on various projects while being a full-time employee, providing stability and the chance to work within a team. Both types will differ depending on the company that hires you, so take it with a grain of salt. One thing to note is that freelance employees typically receive higher pay since they aren't offered benefits like full-time employees. At the start, you may only be able to land one type of job, which is okay. Run with it and keep track of the pluses and negatives of the role.

Dream Big

Thinking beyond your current limitations is crucial when envisioning your desired design role. Consider aspiring to senior roles within design, such as Lead Designer, Senior Designer, Principal Designer, or even Head of Product. These positions come with more responsibility, leadership opportunities, and the chance to shape the direction of a project or organization. Not everyone may want to be a leader and just cruise along as an ordinary designer. Nothing is wrong with that. We ask that you push yourself to be the best in your career, so we are setting the bar high for you. Thank us later!

Examples of Different Roles

Let's explore some examples of these senior design roles to help paint a picture of what they entail and what is achievable:

1. Lead Designer: As a Lead Designer, you would guide and mentor a team of designers. You would oversee the design process, collaborate with stakeholders, and ensure the delivery of high-quality design solutions.
2. Senior Designer: A Senior Designer is an experienced professional who executes design work and provides strategic input. You would be involved in decision-making processes, project planning, and mentoring junior designers.
3. Principal Designer: As a Principal Designer, you would be a design authority within an organization. You would be responsible for setting design standards, driving innovation, and providing thought leadership within the design community.

When you have a goal set, you can make that your one thing to focus on. With that established, in everything you do in your routine, you must think, "Does this align with my one goal?" Keeping your one goal at the top of your mind will help you realize the important things. At times, this may be extremely tough to stick to. Saying no to hanging with friends or shutting yourself in an office to focus will come with hurdles, so make sure you're working for what you want.

To excel in your career path, specific skills and traits are crucial. These include excellent communication and leadership abilities, strategic thinking, a deep understanding of user-centered design principles, and the ability to influence and inspire others. Identifying and developing these skills is critical to working towards your desired role.

Additionally, many years of experience in the field is often necessary to attain these senior roles. While possessing the right skills and traits is essential, employers usually value candidates with a proven track record of success and a wealth of industry knowledge. To give a rough example, mid-level designers have 3–5 years of experience and take on more complex projects. Senior product designers have 5–8 years of experience leading design projects. They may also mentor junior staff and have a say in strategic decisions. If we shoot for the stars, principal designers typically have 8+ years of experience. While this is just a general timeline, and nobody said you can't work your butt off and climb faster if you apply yourself. Just remember Spiderman, “With great power comes great responsibility.”

As you envision your desired design role, setting a time goal for when you want to reach it is essential. A time goal will help you stay focused and motivated on your career path. It's easy to get comfy or become busy with life. Setting a goal date or amount of time you want to work on your goal a day increases your odds of sticking to your guns. It’s all about building good habits and retraining your mind and body.

By envisioning your desired design role, considering different work environments and employment options, and understanding the skills and traits required, you can pave the way for a successful career in design.

WHEN DO YOU WANT TO BE THERE?

In the previous chapters, we explored the various aspects of becoming a designer, focusing on the foundational skills and roles within the field. Now, it's time to delve into the crucial element of envisioning where you want to be in your design career.

Setting goals is essential to career development, providing direction, motivation, and a sense of purpose. By establishing clear objectives, you can create a roadmap to guide you toward your desired role. This chapter will emphasize the significance of goal setting and provide practical insights on achieving your career goals.

Goal Setting

Defining a timeline is a crucial aspect of goal setting. Without a specific timeframe, goals can often become vague and lack the necessary urgency to drive action. Setting a deadline creates a sense of accountability and pushes you to take the necessary steps toward achieving your goals. If you will be working with product managers in the future, you will want to get used to sticking to goals or tasks and knocking them out. You will do it when you work within certain companies and start working with multiple teams. A well-defined timeline helps you stay focused and motivated and provides a clear structure and direction to your efforts, increasing the chances of success.

Tracking your progress is essential for effectively working towards your career goals. Writing down your goals is the first step towards making them tangible and measurable. A written record constantly reminds you of what you're striving for, allowing you to reflect on your achievements and challenges.

When writing down your goals, it's crucial to be specific. Vague goals such as "becoming a better designer" or "landing a high-paying job" lack clarity and make it difficult to measure success. Instead, focus on setting SMART goals - Specific, Measurable, Achievable, Relevant, and Time-bound. It sounds serious, but give it a shot, and don’t let it sway you away. A fantastic and helpful tool is having a daily journal or log. Inside it, write down your goals for the day, week, and weekend. Feel free to track habits or additional things outside this specific journey. Everyone needs to drink more water or take a walk, and those steps are necessary, okay?

While setting goals is essential, it's equally important to acknowledge that setbacks and failures are part of the journey. Only some of your goals may be achieved within the specified timeline, and that's okay. The key is to learn from these experiences and use them as stepping stones towards future success. There will be plenty of moments where you will have to try again or alter your course during this journey and while working after you have landed your career.

Maintaining motivation during challenging times can be tricky. However, by staying focused on your long-term vision and breaking your goals into smaller, manageable tasks, you can overcome obstacles and keep moving forward. Additionally, seeking support from mentors and peers or joining communities of like-minded individuals can provide the encouragement and guidance needed to navigate through setbacks. The goal is to build a village around you of like-minded people; nothing is more motivating than that.

Accountability plays a vital role in achieving your career goals. Sharing your goals with trusted individuals, such as mentors or friends, can help keep you on track and provide valuable feedback and support. Regular check-ins and progress reviews can enhance accountability and ensure you remain committed to your objectives. Heck, if you need a buddy to help with this, you know where to find me.

While staying dedicated to your goals is essential, it's also crucial to recognize when it's time to pivot your strategy. As you progress in your career, circumstances may change, and new opportunities may arise. Being open to reevaluating your goals and adapting your approach can lead to unexpected avenues for growth and advancement. Don’t run yourself ragged and starve your bank accounts because you left all your prior employment for this learning journey. We trust all of you have a good head on your shoulders and understand how to budget your money, so we left that out of this chapter.

As we conclude this chapter on goal setting, it's essential to reflect on the insights shared and start considering the initial steps needed to take action towards your career aspirations. The next chapter will delve into practical strategies for kickstarting your journey, exploring topics such as building a portfolio, networking, and seeking relevant experiences. By combining the knowledge gained from this chapter with the actionable steps in the next, you will be well on your way to your goals!

TAKING THE INITIAL STEPS

Before you cannonball into your design career, it's essential to take the time to explore various topics, skills, and fields to identify what truly resonates with you. This exploration phase will serve as the foundation for your career journey. Take to the online realm of mass information; you can read brilliant articles, watch YouTube, and find educational courses everywhere.

Since you understand who you are and your talents at this point, start connecting the dots when you're exploring educational materials. Connecting those threads makes it easier to decide what you want to do and where you want to be as you envision your end goal.

Researching and Exploring Opportunities

The design world is your oyster, filled with pearls of learning opportunities. Various educational resources are available to suit different learning preferences and budgets. Online platforms like Udemy, Coursera, and Skillshare offer various UX, UI, and product design courses. These courses range from beginner to advanced levels, allowing you to progress at your own pace. Local community colleges and universities often provide more traditional classroom settings for a more structured learning experience. Consider leveraging free resources like Khan Academy (or my resources at danadarr.info) or MIT OpenCourseWare for foundational concepts.

For a more intensive learning journey, boot camps like CareerFoundry, General Assembly, Designlab, or Ironhack offer immersive experiences that can accelerate your understanding and practical skills. These programs often include real-world projects, providing a portfolio upon completion. However, it's essential to thoroughly research and weigh the potential risks and rewards before committing significant time and financial resources. Reading reviews and connecting with alums can offer valuable insights into these programs.

It's crucial to recognize that while formal courses and boot camps provide a solid foundation, they are just the beginning of your learning journey in design.

The field of design is dynamic, and continuous self-education is vital. Engage with the design community on LinkedIn, Dribbble, and Behance platforms. Following industry leaders, joining design groups, and participating in discussions can provide current insights and trends. Consider subscribing to design blogs like Smashing Magazine or A List Apart and listening to podcasts like "99% Invisible" or "Design Matters with Debbie Millman" for deeper industry perspectives.

Remember, every project in the design world is unique and may not adhere strictly to textbook processes. Observe how seasoned designers approach challenges, adapt to trends, and solve problems. Reach out to designers at leading companies, initiate conversations, and ask for feedback on your work. This approach broadens your understanding and helps build a professional network in the industry.

In summary, structured courses and boot camps are valuable but merely a starting point. To excel in your design career, embrace a mindset of continuous learning and active participation in the design community.

Once you understand the design landscape better and know how or where you want to learn, it's time to conduct in-depth research and immerse yourself in the field you are most interested in. Stick to the subject you found most exciting and go out there to gain valuable knowledge about the type of design work you want to pursue. For example, if designing pretty things and maintaining a design library sounds fun, dig into UI design and start looking into how enterprise companies run their design systems to learn best practices. If you love strategy, you may be a gamer. Start a UX course and understand how top UX designers dissolve large-scale product problems with their design solutions. It will surprise you how much we have learned from our previous chapters, which will start to tie into what you're learning.

Refining your Focus

As you delve deeper into your design education and explorations, refining your focus and committing to a specific area of expertise becomes crucial. This process, known as "niching down," is a pivotal step in your learning journey. Whether your interest lies in UI design, UX research, or broader product design, dedicating yourself to one specific field can significantly enhance your learning efficiency and expertise.

Consider further specializing within your chosen niche. For instance, if you're drawn to UX, you might focus on UX writing or user research. If UI is your passion, delve into UI design libraries or specialize in creating high-converting landing pages for e-commerce. This level of focus allows for deeper learning and mastery, enabling you to become a sought-after expert in a particular facet of design.

Another strategy is to set a "time box" for this phase of your journey. Decide on a realistic timeframe for how long you will dedicate yourself to mastering this niche. This time frame could range from several months to a few years, depending on your goals, previous experience, and the complexity of the field. A time box acts as a structured guide, motivating and helping you remain accountable in your learning process.

It's important to remember that mastering a design discipline is a marathon, not a sprint. While some may find footing quickly, for others, it may take years to educate themselves and secure their ideal design role fully. Be patient with your progress, keep an open mind, and remember that this dedicated period of focused learning is a valuable investment in your future career.

Embracing Patience

It's important to remember that building new career skills takes time and effort. Just like building a six-pack at the gym, it's a gradual process that requires patience and consistency. Just don't let that hard work turn into stubbornness. If you need to pivot, do so. Suppose you can't pay rent because you are overarching and trying to learn everything. Know that and adjust yourself. Get used to shifting because, as a designer, that is an essential skill. Understand that you will discover some things over time and embrace the learning curve as an integral part of your growth. Each small step you take brings you closer to becoming a proficient designer.

Realistically, getting into consistent work can take months and sometimes years. We have this guide and stress-specific points to start early in your journey. For example, this chapter is about narrowing down, studying what you enjoy, and becoming the best you can be. If you genuinely find something you love, it will show, and that will land you work.

Now that you have laid the groundwork for your design career, it's time to delve deeper into your chosen niche. The next chapter will explore the importance of sticking with a niche and how it can propel your career forward. You will gain expertise and differentiate yourself in the competitive design industry by specializing in a specific area. Get ready to discover practical strategies for honing your skills and thriving in your chosen niche.

EXPLORING NICHE & BRAND

In the previous chapter, we discussed the benefits of specializing in a specific design area rather than trying to be a jack-of-all-trades. Now, we will reaffirm why being great at one skill is better than being a jack of all trades. Delve deep into that skill and become highly experienced when zeroing in on a particular niche. You can develop expertise that sets you apart by dedicating your time and effort to mastering a specific area. The goal is to stand out in the massive sea of designers looking for work, right?

Embracing Your Expertise and Overcoming Hurdles

For this example, let us say you have chosen to have a powerhouse analytical brain and want to work as a UX researcher. You have always been good at reading people. Maybe you took some psychology classes or worked in customer service for eight years and know how to read people like a book. You may hit hurdles or doubts while mastering being a researcher.

Now, in a universe where everyone seems to be a jack-of-all-trades (and master of none), there's a secret weapon called specialization. By focusing laser-like on UX research, you're not just another face in the designer crowd; you're the go-to guru, the wizard of user insights! It's like being the person at a party who can name every cheese on the platter – oddly specific but impressive and sought-after.

Specializing means you can wave goodbye to job listings that expect you to be a designer, coder, office barista, and part-time wizard all rolled into one. Instead, you become the hero in your niche—a beacon of knowledge that clients and opportunities flock to. Think of it as a human magnet for cool gigs that let you flex your brain muscles and maybe even pay enough for that fancy ergonomic chair.

It's common to experience imposter syndrome—a feeling of self-doubt and inadequacy despite your accomplishments. It's essential to believe in yourself and the skills you're learning. Remember that expertise is not acquired overnight; it takes time, patience, and practice. It's common to face this adversary even when you are a well-trained veteran. Get comfortable with feeling uncomfortable.

To overcome imposter syndrome, remember you have put in the blood, sweat, and tears to acquire new skills. Okay, no blood, but maybe some sweat and tears. Embrace that you are talented and have experience in your niche, and acknowledge the value you bring. Surround yourself with a supportive community of like-minded individuals who can encourage and help guide you. The power of like-minded individuals' influence draws back into the power of networking. Supportive communities are everything as you build yourself. Surround yourself with people who are in the place where you want to be. Who is in your immediate circle now, and do they support who you want to become? Chew on that if you haven't done so before.

Building Your Brand

Now that you're on the path to honing your skills in your chosen niche, it's time to create your branding. Your brand is a powerful tool that helps you showcase your expertise and attract the right clients or job opportunities.

First, let's discuss your unique value proposition (UVP). UVP isn't just corporate jargon; it's the secret sauce that makes you, well, you. It's about that unique flavor you bring to the table – maybe it's your knack for creating user-friendly designs or your ability to turn data into stunning visuals. Like a good cup of coffee, your UVP should leave a strong, lasting impression. If you're feeling stuck, consider this: your journey towards mastering your niche is a story worth telling. Imagine you're at a superhero convention – what story sets you apart from the rest?

Creating a brand can feel as daunting as writing a dating profile. It's personal, a bit awkward, but essential. Why not turn to your friends or colleagues if you're hitting a wall? It's okay to lean on others or borrow ideas as you build your identity. Not everyone is going to be a master out of the gate. A great goal to set here is to come up with your elevator pitch. What can you say to someone in a minute or so that will sell you and your skills?

In addition to your brand story, it's crucial to establish a consistent visual identity that reflects your niche and resonates with your target audience. Your identity includes elements like your logo, color scheme, and overall design aesthetic. You will create a memorable and professional impression with a cohesive visual identity. People will see what is on the outside first, and while this may be unfortunate, we should do our best to present ourselves the best we can. Something to remember: People will see great UI and think this makes for a great user experience. It is essential to realize how people feel when viewing your profile online. Consider how we may see someone dressed in a suit and tie and assume they're imperative or a business person. We judge with the first sense, and that is typically sight.

Leveraging online platforms such as a website or social media can significantly enhance your personal branding efforts. These platforms allow you to showcase your portfolio, share insights, and engage with the design community. By actively participating in these online communities, you can establish yourself as an expert in your field and build valuable connections. Some examples of this could be posting insights and tips on LinkedIn; another could be posting to TikTok or Instagram if you enjoy that. We have seen designers not even need a portfolio to leverage social media, but that is a non-traditional route that takes pure dedication. The point is to get your name out there and advocate yourself. Anything you can do to put yourself out there will be helpful in your journey. Decide where you want to spend your energy.

In conclusion, creating a solid personal brand is essential for showcasing your expertise and attracting the right clients or job opportunities. By defining your unique value proposition, crafting a compelling brand story, establishing a consistent visual identity, and leveraging online platforms, you can effectively communicate your skills and stand out in your chosen niche.

In summary, a solid personal brand is your ally in showcasing your expertise and attracting the right opportunities. Your UVP, brand story, visual identity, and online presence are the tools you need to stand out in your chosen niche. Remember, settling into your niche is just the start. Keep learning, stay curious, and you'll continue to grow as a designer. Next, we'll dive into the toolkit you'll need to keep evolving and thriving in your design journey. Stay tuned and remember – every superhero has a beginning.

PATHS TO MASTERY

This chapter will explore various learning resources for aspiring UI, UX, and product designers and provide a comprehensive guide to online and offline resources catering to different learning styles and needs. To become a proficient designer, one must immerse oneself in a rich learning environment. This chapter delves into various resources that offer the knowledge and skills necessary to excel in these fields.

Online Learning Resources:

1. Bootcamp Style Courses: Look online for CareerFoundry, Springboard, General Assembly, or Designlab.
2. Coursera and Udemy Courses:
    a. UI Design Specialization: Learn the fundamentals of user interface design, including design principles, typography, and color theory.
    b. UX Design Fundamentals: This course offers insights into user experience design, focusing on understanding user needs and creating intuitive, user-friendly designs.
    c. Product Design and Development: A comprehensive course that blends UI/UX principles with product management skills.
3. Skillshare Classes: Explore a range of classes taught by industry professionals, offering practical projects and real-world insights in design.
4. YouTube Channels: 'The Futur' and 'AJ&Smart' provide accessible, high-quality content on design thinking, case studies, and industry trends.
5. Design Blogs and Websites: Smashing Magazine, UX Design.cc, and Behance offer articles, tutorials, and showcases of innovative design work.

Offline Learning Resources:

1. Workshops and Seminars: Participate in local workshops and seminars conducted by design schools or community centers, which offer hands-on experience and networking opportunities.
2. Design Conferences: Attend international design conferences like Adobe MAX or UX Week to gain insights from leading professionals and connect with fellow designers.
3. University Courses and Degrees: For a more structured and in-depth learning experience, consider enrolling in a bachelor's or master's program in graphic design, human-computer interaction, or a related field.
4. Local Design Communities: Join local design groups or meetups to engage in discussions, collaborate on projects, and share experiences with other aspiring designers. Try the Meetup app or search for Hackathons near you or online.

This list is to get the juices pumping, but it doesn't cover everything. It's a handbook, not Google. Find something that you find exciting and retain the information from. Some of these courses will offer certificates; if that is something you want, find the correct course that suits your needs. Some boot camps offer a career guarantee. Keep an eye out for the fine print, folks! Do your best here, but try not to waste too much time in analysis paralysis when picking a patch to start down.

DESIGN TOOLS

Your chosen tools and software can significantly shape your workflow and creative output in the ever-evolving design world. This chapter will discuss the most common design tools and software used by designers, explaining why they're used, which type of designer typically uses each tool and the importance of mastering these tools. Additionally, we will explore the reasons for focusing on a single tool rather than learning many. There it is again, singling down and niching—a common thread throughout this book.

The Design Tools Landscape

In the ever-evolving design world, staying abreast of the latest tools is crucial for professionals across various disciplines. As of 2023, the landscape of design tools has seen some exciting developments, catering to the nuanced needs of UI, UX, and product designers.

In a way, Figma has become the 'cool kid on the block' in the software design world for UX, UI, or product designers. It's like the Swiss Army knife of design tools, offering collaborative capabilities that make teamwork look as easy as pie. Other competitors are out there, such as Adobe XD and Sketch, which are all very similar. We suggest going with what you can use and enjoy using here. Second, look at what the bulk of companies use for their tools out there and use that tool. In the worst case, most of these tools are similar, and transitioning around isn't impossible.

Adobe Photoshop remains an industry mainstay for graphic designers, celebrated for its unparalleled image editing and compositing features. However, the rise of alternatives like Affinity Photo and Procreate, especially for tablet users, offers more choices for creatives seeking versatility and mobility. Meanwhile, vector-based design software such as Adobe Illustrator and the increasingly popular Vectornator is essential for creating scalable graphics, from logos to detailed illustrations. Job listings may ask you to be familiar with Adobe Suite products, such as these, and decide if this is your desired career. If you want to create pretty things such as logos or handle brand design, then Adobe products may be the way for you.

When mastering these magical tools, designers often face the 'specialization vs. diversification' conundrum. Do you want to be the Gandalf of Figma or the jack-of-all-trades in the design tool realm? Specializing lets you dive deep – you'll know your chosen tool like the back of your hand. But are you diversifying? That's like having a Swiss Army knife in a wilderness survival scenario – handy in many situations. However, 2023 is all about the hybrid approach. It's like being a decathlete in design – have a primary tool you can wield like a lightsaber, but don't be clueless about the rest.

However, in 2023, the trend leans towards a hybrid approach. Designers are encouraged to have a strong command of one primary tool while maintaining a working knowledge of others. This approach ensures depth in skill while allowing flexibility to adapt to different project needs or team environments.

The internet offers many resources for those looking to learn or enhance their skills. Platforms like LinkedIn Learning, Skillshare, and Udemy host extensive courses on virtually every design tool. These platforms often feature courses taught by industry professionals and provide practical, project-based learning experiences. Many tool-specific websites, such as the Adobe Creative Cloud tutorials, offer free resources and guides to help users of all levels. Community forums and YouTube channels also serve as valuable resources for tips, tricks, and tutorials, catering to beginners and advanced users.

Incorporating AI Tools in the Design Process

In addition to the landscape of traditional design tools, the emergence and integration of AI tools will become a significant trend in 2023, offering new possibilities and efficiencies for designers across all disciplines. Be mindful of what you use, as many AI products are still being tested and are incapable of taking on everything you must throw at them. At the current time of writing this, they work well to speed up some processes but do not do your job for you. Luckily, the robots haven't taken over just yet!

UI and graphic-based designers can leverage AI tools for tasks such as image generation, color palette suggestions, and layout design. Tools like Adobe's Sensei use AI to automate and enhance specific tasks, like object selection and image resizing, allowing designers to focus on creative aspects. AI-driven platforms like Canvas Magic Resize and Looka for logo creation are also gaining popularity for their ease of use and time-saving capabilities.

For UI/UX designers, AI can play a pivotal role in user testing and data analysis. Tools like Google Analytics and Hotjar now incorporate AI to provide deeper insights into user behavior. AI can also assist in creating more personalized user experiences. Platforms like Uizard use AI to transform hand-drawn sketches into digital designs, speeding up the prototyping process.

Product designers find AI particularly useful for predicting user preferences and market trends. AI tools can analyze large datasets to inform design decisions, ensuring products meet consumer needs. For example, Autodesk's generative design software uses AI to create optimized designs based on specified goals and constraints, revolutionizing product conception.

Tips for integrating AI:

1. Start Small: Integrate AI tools into minor aspects of your projects to understand their capabilities. Use AI for color selection, layout adjustments, or essential prototyping.
2. Stay Informed: Keep abreast of your field's latest AI tools and updates. Follow design blogs, attend webinars, and participate in online forums to learn how others use AI effectively.
3. Balance AI and Creativity: While AI can enhance efficiency, remember that the core of design lies in creativity and human insight. Use AI to complement, not replace, your creative process.
4. Understand Data Privacy: When using AI tools, especially in UX design, consider user data privacy and ethical considerations. Ensure that your use of AI aligns with legal standards and moral best practices.
5. Experiment and Learn: Don't hesitate to experiment with different AI tools to see which ones best fit your workflow. Learning by doing is often the most effective way to understand how AI can benefit your design process.

In summary, the choice of tools in a designer's arsenal is crucial and should align with their specialization, the demands of the industry, and their personal workflow preferences. With a multitude of online resources available, learning and mastering these tools has become more accessible than ever before. The key is to stay curious, continually learn, and adapt to the changing landscape of design tools and technology.

DON'T WAIT, START NETWORKING

Throughout this guide, we discussed the importance of networking, akin to finding the golden snitch in a game of Quidditch and understanding why networking isn't just a buzzword but a crucial ladder in building your career. Whether you're an extrovert who thrives in crowds or an introvert who prefers the cozy corner of a coffee shop, this chapter is your guide to making connections that count. Please start thinking about your most significant challenge with networking so we can tackle this together.

The Bedrock of Your Career: Networking

Networking is more than just exchanging business cards or adding connections on LinkedIn. It's about building relationships that can guide, inspire, and open doors for you throughout your career. Think of it as planting seeds; some might sprout immediately, providing quick opportunities or advice, while others may take time to grow, leading to long-term collaborations or mentorships. In the design industry, where trends and technologies change as fast as fashion in Milan, staying connected keeps you informed and relevant. It's like having a backstage pass to the concert of the design world – you get to see the real action, not just the highlight reel.

Moreover, networking isn't just about what you can get but what you can give. It's a two-way street where sharing your knowledge and resources can establish you as a credible and valuable community member. Think about networking, like making new friends, offering what you can, and not expecting something in return. Remember, in a field as collaborative as design, your next big break could come from a recommendation or insight gained through your network.

Waiting to build your network until you think you're "ready" or until it's "too late" is like waiting to eat your popcorn until the movie ends – pointless and unsatisfying. Begin your networking journey at the onset of your career-hunting journey. As a budding designer, connecting with peers and professionals can provide resources and guidance. It's like having a map when you're navigating a new city. These early connections can offer feedback on your work, suggest learning resources, and even point you toward job opportunities. Starting early also means you grow your network as you grow in your career. By the time you're a seasoned designer, you'll have a galaxy of connections, each with its own set of experiences and insights. Plus, networking isn't a one-off task; it's a garden that needs regular tending. Begin early, and you'll have a lush garden when required.

Introvert Tactics

The digital world is your ally for introverts who might view networking like a cat views a bath. Online networks offer a platform to connect without the overwhelming sensory experiences of in-person events. Platforms like LinkedIn, design forums, and social media groups allow you to engage at your own pace, in your own space.

Leveraging online networks also means you can tailor your interactions. You can join groups specific to your interests, participate in discussions, and even showcase your work to a global audience. Online networking can often feel more like sharing a conversation over coffee than shouting in a crowded room. Plus, it offers the luxury of thought-out responses and the ability to exit with the click of a button. Start building your LinkedIn profile and searching for fellow designers who work at the places you want to be, do the types of work you want to do, or are active in the online design community. Whenever you add someone, leave them a note, and don't be a faceless connection.

However, while online networking is a powerful tool, something must be said about the magic of face-to-face interactions. If you're an introvert, attending a networking event might feel like being thrown into the deep end. But remember, growth often happens outside our comfort zones. Start small – attend a local meetup or a seminar. Prepare some talking points beforehand, like discussing a recent project you're proud of or a design trend you're interested in. It's like having a cheat sheet in a test.

Networking as an introvert doesn't mean changing who you are; it's about leveraging your strengths. Introverts are often great listeners and thoughtful conversationalists—two skills that are gold in networking. Aim to make genuine connections rather than collecting contacts. It's not about the quantity of connections you make but the quality.

CREATING A PORTFOLIO

A portfolio is to a designer what a wand is to a wizard - it's essential. In this chapter, we'll explore the why's and how's of building a portfolio that showcases your work and tells your story as a designer. From the traditional digital portfolio to the innovative use of social media, we'll cover all bases. Plus, we'll guide you through resources and platforms to build your portfolio and show you the importance of continuous feedback and improvement.

For designers, a portfolio is more than a collection of work; it's a narrative of your skills, style, and journey. It's the first thing potential employers, clients, or collaborators will look for. A well-crafted portfolio demonstrates not just the final product but also your thought process, problem-solving skills, and adaptability to various projects. It's like your personal museum, where each piece tells a unique story of your creativity and expertise. In a field as dynamic as design, your portfolio is the anchor that grounds your talents and showcases your evolution.

Moreover, a portfolio is a living document of your professional journey. It's not just about what you've done but a testament to where you can go. It's your brand, visual resume, and, in many cases, your first impression. In a world where images often speak louder than words, your portfolio is your voice.

Need help with your case study? Here is a link to my free resources. danadarr.info

Social Media as an Alternative Portfolio

In the digital age, some designers turn to social media as an alternative to a traditional portfolio. Platforms like Instagram, Behance, or Pinterest can act as dynamic, easily accessible showcases of your work. However, this route demands a different level of effort – you're displaying your work and engaging an audience. Social media portfolios need regular updates, consistent themes, and engagement with followers. It's like throwing a party; you must keep the guests entertained and interested.

While social media can increase your visibility and provide a more informal way to show your work, it often needs more depth and detail than a traditional portfolio. It's great for catching eyes but might not capture the comprehensive journey of your design process. Think of it as the trailer to your movie – exciting and engaging, but not the whole story. Decide if this works for you, and remember if you're an introvert and want to do this. You can. Plenty of channels have "faceless" content. You can utilize screen recording, different videos, and photos.

Learning About Portfolio Creation

For those who need help figuring out where to start, numerous resources are available to help you create a compelling portfolio—websites like AIGA and HOW to offer articles and guides on portfolio design. In comparison, online courses on platforms like Skillshare or Udemy provide step-by-step instructions and examples. If you could have taken courses previously in your journey, such as a boot camp or college courses, you may have gone over this and started your portfolio already (give yourself a pat on the back). These resources cover everything from selecting your best work to presenting it cohesively. A short Google search can unlock the world of portfolios, so we shouldn't struggle too much to find learning resources today. If you want direct guidance, shoot a message on LinkedIn.

Books like "Building a Portfolio that Will Get You Hired" by David Sherwin or "How to Create a Portfolio and Get Hired" by Fig Taylor also offer valuable insights into crafting a portfolio that stands out. Remember, learning about portfolio creation is not a one-time task – it's an ongoing process as you grow and evolve as a designer. Many have entirely restarted their portfolios as our experience or ideology changes. Just roll with it and present your best self to the world.

Platforms for Your Portfolio

Several user-friendly websites cater specifically to designers when building and hosting your portfolio. Uxfolio, Squarespace, Wix, and Weebly offer customizable templates and easy-to-use interfaces for those less tech-savvy. For more control and customization, platforms like Webflow, WordPress, or Adobe Portfolio can be excellent choices. Behance and Dribbble are also popular among designers who do not host portfolios, as well as the community and exposure they offer. You will typically see more UI and graphic designers using the last two options, so whatever your choice is, remember you can always pivot later. Just pick a direction and fly with it!

Each platform has pros and cons, so it's worth exploring to see which aligns best with your needs and skills. Think of your portfolio platform as your stage – it should complement and enhance your performance, not overshadow it.

Once your portfolio is up and running, it's time to unleash it into the wild and brace yourself for feedback. Have mentors, peers, or even potential clients review your portfolio. This feedback is invaluable as it provides fresh perspectives and can highlight strengths and weaknesses you might have yet to notice. It's like having a test audience for a new movie – their reactions can guide your edits.

Continuously update your portfolio with new case studies and projects as you finish them. Regular updates show your progression and keep your portfolio fresh and relevant. A portfolio is never truly 'finished' – it's a living, evolving showcase of your journey as a designer. Remember to highlight your best projects; you can deprecate old work when you bring in new work. Try to keep three to six projects in your portfolio. Many new designers will have one to three personal projects on theirs. It can be easy to tell when someone is a newbie that way or if they're all personal and not professional projects. Try to keep your projects polished as if they're professional. You can always find people to work with for free and start a case study group since you should be networking throughout this process.

In our next chapter, we'll explore the art of creating compelling case studies, which are the heartbeats of your portfolio. We'll discuss spinning your design process into a captivating narrative and presenting your solutions in a way that makes readers sit up, take notice, and maybe even give you a standing ovation.

CREATING A CASE STUDY

This chapter will guide you through the essential steps of creating a compelling case study, from outlining your story to engagingly presenting your deliverables. We'll also explore how to draw inspiration from existing case studies, choose suitable projects for your case study, and the importance of continually updating your work.

Now, let's talk about how to find inspiration. Taking out your magnifying glass and investigating what others are doing is okay. We will call this "creative borrowing." Take time to study other case studies. Look at how other designers structure their content, the types of visuals they use, and how they weave their stories. Platforms like Google, Behance, Medium, or LinkedIn can be goldmines for such research. Notice the commonalities – these are often tried-and-true techniques that resonate with audiences.

However, while drawing inspiration from others is beneficial, remember to infuse your unique style and approach. It's okay to "creatively borrow" elements that work but constantly tailor them to fit your narrative and brand. Your case study should reflect you as a designer, showcasing your skills and individuality.

Ideating what project to use for your case study can be challenging. You can start with projects from your job or a volunteer project or even address a problem in your personal life. The key is to select a project that showcases a breadth of your skills and thinking process. It's not always about the project's complexity but the depth of your approach.

If you're starting, don't abandon hypothetical projects or redesigns. These can be great ways to demonstrate your creativity and ability to identify and solve design problems. If you have school or boot camp projects, this is the perfect time to revisit and refine them. Your growth as a designer should be evident in how you evolve and improve upon past work.

Before diving into the visual elements, start with an outline. An outline is the backbone of your case study, where you sketch out the narrative. Begin by defining the problem you addressed and the initial proposed solution. What was the challenge? Who was it for? Doing this upfront sets the stage for your story. Next, detail your process - the brainstorming, the iterations, and the decision-making journey. How did you arrive at your solution?

Be mindful that hiring managers or recruiters will be scanning your content. The more oversized typography should lead them through critical points like a highlight reel. Don't add content that says, "We held user interviews because it helped us get insights." Update it and highlight the impact, insights, or metrics. "We held three interviews and found 80% of users left the journey during onboarding." When someone scans your content, it sounds cleaner and easier to understand. The sub-copy below can delve into your process more, but keep it trimmed. We don't need a book the size of Harry Potter and the Goblet of Fire underneath your headings.

After outlining the problem and process, focus on the outcome. What was the solution? It could have changed from the original solution, so you can explain why. How did it impact the user or the client? Flexing your outcome is your chance to showcase the results and effectiveness of your design. Remember, a good case study is like a good story - it has a beginning (the problem), a middle (the process), and an end (the solution). Your outline should be clear, concise, and structured, laying a solid foundation for your case study.

Once your outline is in place, it's time to embellish it with your deliverables—the visual proof of your work. The visuals can include sketches, wireframes, mockups, or even prototypes. But remember, this step is about more than just aesthetics; it's about clarity and context. Your visuals should be attractive, informative, and relevant to the narrative of your case study.

As you integrate these elements, ensure they enhance and support your story. Each visual should add value, demonstrating a particular aspect of your process or solution. Think of your deliverables as characters in your story – each has a role and contributes to the overall narrative. Be mindful of the layout and flow; your case study should be easy to follow and engaging, leading the viewer naturally from one point to the next.

Deliverables should be polished past their original form if they weren't in original work. For example, add those wireframes into a laptop mockup or Google Chrome browser to make things realistic. Annotate specific points in the deliverable so readers know where to focus and what was found at that point. Maybe you found that the UI of a webpage was not accessible for the colorblind, and you want to focus on the buttons or CTAs on a page.

Picture your case study as a plant. Not just any plant, but one of those tricky bonsai trees that need constant pruning and care. As you grow and evolve in your design journey, so should your case studies. Revisit them like you would an old friend. Update them with new insights and sprinkle in improved visuals. At some point, you may feel sick and tired of looking at this thing, and that's perfectly normal. It's okay to take breaks and return to this. We all need to take a break occasionally.

Now, let's talk about feedback – the secret sauce of improvement. Share your case studies with mentors and peers, or bravely venture into the wild jungles of places like LinkedIn. Yes, it might feel like feeding your work to the lions, but constructive criticism is like a treasure map – it guides you to uncharted territories of excellence. Get comfortable with throwing yourself "in the fire," and if you can't seem to do it, find others who push you to do uncomfortable things. This is how you will grow, as much as some of us may hate to admit.

Strap in for the next chapter, where we'll leap into the world of finding work. It's time to flex those creative muscles you've nurtured like a gym bro on New Year's Day. We'll explore how to harness the power of your network, which you've been building up like a social media influencer. Get ready to turn those connections into opportunities and start strutting your stuff on the design runway!

UTILIZE YOUR NETWORK TO FIND VOLUNTEER WORK

In previous chapters, we've emphasized the importance of networking. Let's extend that conversation by exploring how your network can be a goldmine for finding volunteer opportunities. Volunteering is not just about lending a helping hand; it's a strategic move for gaining real-world experience, building your portfolio, and even paving the way to paid work. In this chapter, we'll navigate the avenues for finding these opportunities, including online communities, and discuss the value of volunteer work in your professional growth.

Tapping into Your Network for Opportunities

Your network, built through the strategies discussed in previous chapters, is a rich resource for uncovering volunteer opportunities. As we have hinted, networking isn't a one-way street; it's about building relationships. Engage with your connections on platforms like LinkedIn or ADPList, not just when you need something but as part of an ongoing conversation. Share your interest in finding volunteer work, and be clear about the skills you can offer and the experiences you're seeking.

These platforms are not just for job hunting; they're communities where opportunities like volunteer projects will be found. LinkedIn, for example, has specific groups and posts dedicated to volunteer work. ADPList provides mentors who might know of such opportunities. Remember, the key is to be proactive. Reach out to connections, participate in discussions, and make your intentions known.

Volunteer work can often be the stepping stone to paid opportunities. It's a chance to showcase your skills, work ethic, and adaptability in a real-world setting. Through volunteering, you demonstrate your value, which can lead to job offers or referrals. It's like a test drive for potential employers or clients – they see your skills in action. These projects may be with real-world clients. It's possible they need help, and you or your team can offer your skills for free. Stay within reason, and be clear with the goals of a volunteer project; you don't want to get stuck with a never-ending amount of work.

Volunteering can fill gaps in your resume, provide substantial content for your portfolio, and give you stories to share in job interviews. It's about building a track record and gaining confidence in your abilities. Treat these opportunities as you would a paid project - with professionalism and dedication. The impression you make can open doors to future paid work. It can lead to a richer, more diverse portfolio, showcasing your versatility as a designer. And let's remember the personal satisfaction and growth that comes from contributing to a cause or helping an organization. How many more reasons do you need?

In addition to LinkedIn and ADPList, explore Slack and Discord communities related to design. These platforms host many groups where designers share resources, opportunities, and support. Joining these groups can lead to volunteer opportunities and provide a space for learning and networking. Engage in these communities – participate in discussions, offer insights, and be open to new connections.

These online communities are also excellent for staying updated on industry trends and events. Many communities host virtual meetups, workshops, and informal chats. All of these can be great for networking and finding volunteer opportunities. Remember, your active participation is vital. The more you engage, the more visible you become to potential collaborators.

Volunteer projects can often offer more creative freedom and the opportunity to experiment and explore new areas of design. They can also lead to a richer, more diverse portfolio, showcasing your versatility as a designer. And let's remember the personal satisfaction and growth that comes from contributing to a cause or helping an organization.

In the next chapter, we'll pivot to personal branding. We'll explore how to create a brand that resonates with your values and goals and how to effectively communicate your unique identity as a designer in the marketplace.

BUILDING YOUR BRAND

In a world filled with talented designers, your brand sets you apart. It's your signature, your mark in the design landscape. This chapter delves into the essence of building a personal brand as a designer, the practical uses of a strong brand, maintaining brand cohesiveness, and harnessing your unique traits to shape your brand. We'll explore how a well-crafted brand can open doors to other forms of income and presence in the digital world.

Personal Brand for Designers

A personal brand is more than a logo or a color scheme; it represents who you are, what you stand for, and what you bring to the table. It's your story, your values, and your style, all wrapped into one cohesive narrative. For designers, this is particularly crucial. Your brand reflects your design philosophy, problem-solving approach, and aesthetic sensibilities. It's what potential clients or employers remember about you, and it's often the deciding factor in getting that project or job.

For designers, your brand is like your fashion statement in the design world. It mirrors your design philosophy, approach to untangling the knot of design problems, and aesthetic charm. It's what sticks in the minds of clients or employers.

Your brand is a versatile tool. It's not just for attracting clients or employers; it's also for building your network, establishing credibility in your field, and even branching out into other areas such as teaching, speaking, or writing. Your brand is like a key that can unlock multiple doors.

When your brand hits the right chord with people, it's like opening the floodgates to Collaborationville. We're talking partnerships, joint ventures, and your fan club. It can be a soapbox for championing the causes close to your heart or the captain's wheel steering industry initiatives. A well-crafted brand doesn't just give you a seat at the table; it gives you a megaphone to voice your ideas, influence the design universe, and sprinkle a little bit of your magic in the community.

Consistency is key in branding. Your brand should be cohesive across all platforms – from your social media profiles to your portfolio and email signature. This consistency reinforces your brand identity and makes it easier for people to recognize and remember you. Think of it like a theme song; no matter where you hear it, you instantly recognize it.

Your color scheme, typography, tone of voice, and visual elements should be consistent across your digital presence. Consistency creates a seamless experience for anyone interacting with your brand, whether on LinkedIn, Instagram, or your website. Consistency in branding builds a strong, recognizable, and professional image.

Building your brand doesn't require complex strategies. It can start with who you are—your personality, style, or unique professional traits. Are you a minimalist designer who loves clean lines and muted colors? Or are you vibrant, bold, and unafraid to use color and patterns? Your brand can reflect these elements. It's okay to be shiny and loud or minimal and impactful.

Leveraging Your Brand for Growth

Once you have established your brand and online presence, there are numerous ways to leverage it. You can start a blog, a social media, or even a podcast, sharing your insights and experiences in design. Sharing your insights reinforces your brand and can become a source of income through advertising, sponsorships, or affiliate marketing.

Your brand can also lead to opportunities such as speaking engagements, workshops, or guest appearances on panels. These platforms broaden your network and establish you as an authority in your field. When nurtured and leveraged correctly, your brand can become a robust career growth and diversification tool. This notion may rock your boat and be far beyond where you want to go. Go back to your goal setting, where you put your end goal, and think if utilizing methods like this will get you where you want to be.

In the next episode, we'll explore the art of showcasing your work and seeking feedback. We'll discuss the platforms and strategies for presenting your work effectively and how to use the feedback received for continuous improvement and growth in your design journey.

BE BRAVE, SHOW OFF YOUR WORK

In the journey of a designer, creating work is only half the battle; the other half is showing it off. This chapter is all about the courage to showcase your work, gather feedback, and embrace the process of growth and improvement. We call this "throwing yourself into the fire." Whether through your network, strangers, or online platforms, each avenue offers valuable insights that can refine your skills and bolster your confidence. We want to make our projects stronger than Hercules himself. We'll explore the importance of feedback, the art of handling criticism, and tips for introverts to navigate this process. By the end of this chapter, you'll be ready to put your work out there boldly and take the following steps toward your dream career.

Gathering Feedback

Feedback is the breakfast of champions, especially for designers. Your network, comprising mentors, peers, and colleagues, is a treasure trove of wisdom and insight. They know you and your journey; they understand your strengths and areas for growth. Presenting your work to them allows for constructive, tailored feedback that can significantly refine your design approach and execution. The advantage of feedback from your network is that trust and understanding are already established. These individuals are invested in your growth and can provide specific, actionable advice. Their feedback often comes from experience and knowledge about the industry, making it particularly valuable. Starting with your network is also easier if you aren't comfortable speaking to strangers. Putting yourself out there isn't easy.

Strap in for a wild ride because feedback from strangers is like jumping into the deep end of the design pool – it pushes you out of your cozy comfort zone and straight into the real world. They provide a fresh, unbiased perspective and often point out things that those familiar with your work might overlook. Sharing your work on platforms outside your immediate network, such as online design communities, forums, or social media platforms like LinkedIn and Dribbble, exposes you to a broader audience with diverse viewpoints.

Now, let's fast-forward a bit. Picture yourself in the not-so-distant future, showcasing your work to coworkers and stakeholders or in the nerve-wracking arena of job interviews. It's like a talent show where the judges are your future colleagues; every critique is a step toward your standing ovation. The more you practice now – diving headfirst into the feedback pool – the better you'll swim in these big-league waters. So, embrace the feedback, even the tricky bits. It's the designer's spinach – it might not always taste great, but it makes you stronger!

Posting your work online is more than just sharing; it's a declaration of your presence in the design world. Each platform has its unique audience and style of interaction. LinkedIn can connect you with professionals and potential employers, while Dribbble and Behance are more about creativity and design feedback. Regularly posting your work online keeps your portfolio fresh and relevant, and it helps build an audience for your design voice and style.

Vulnerability and Criticism

Stepping into the spotlight with your work is like doing a high-wire act without a net – a brave show of vulnerability. You're not just displaying your designs; you're opening the floor to criticism, which, let's face it, can sometimes feel like juggling pineapples – a bit prickly and unpredictable. But here's the thing: this openness to critique is vital. Whether it's presenting to clients, colleagues, or the digital audience of public forums, getting cozy with sharing your work is critical prep for the big league.

Aim for constructive feedback – the kind that shapes and sculpts your skills. Think of criticism like a treasure hunt. Not every comment is a gem, but buried within are insights that can polish your design prowess. Learning to sift through feedback is an art that refines you as a designer. If you receive a full page of corrections on something, realize that you don't need to adhere to everything on this list as it's the opinion of another. It's up to you to make the final judgment, and if you are wondering what to do, follow up!

For introverts, broadcasting your work is as appealing as singing karaoke in a crowded room. Start small. Share your creations in cozy online groups where you feel at home. Foster connections with mentors or find digital pals who offer a cushioned landing for your first forays into the world of feedback. This is why we mentioned building your networking before this step, giving you time to get comfy for things like this.

Harness the power of the internet. Your remote control allows you to dictate the pace and scale of your exposure. Begin with platforms that feel more like a friendly chat over coffee rather than a spotlight on a stage. Remember, feedback isn't a measure of your worth as a human or an artist; it's a stepping stone on your path to growth. You're building your skills and confidence with each piece of work you share and each critique you absorb. Before you know it, you'll be ready to take on the world – or at least a more significant online forum (like the CEO of your new dream job).

Showcasing your work and gathering feedback is vital to your growth as a designer. It builds confidence, exposes you to different perspectives, and hones your ability to handle criticism constructively. As you step out of your comfort zone and embrace this process, remember that each piece of feedback is a stepping stone to becoming a better designer. One last little nugget to remember whenever you make a design decision or choose to pivot your path with your work. It is pivotal that you have a reason to back it up. It's never an excuse to say, "Ugh, I don't know, I just did it because it looked cool."

In the next chapter, we'll shift gears to applying for jobs. We'll use the foundations laid in networking, building your brand, creating your portfolio, and showcasing your work to navigate the job market and land paid work. It's time to take everything you've learned and translate it into tangible career success.

APPLYING FOR JOBS

In this chapter, we dive into the tactical phase of your design journey: applying for jobs. Applying for work is where all your hard work culminates, from networking to portfolio building. We'll explore setting realistic job-hunting goals, effective methods to track these goals, tools, and strategies for the job search, and how to present yourself to potential employers. We'll also discuss handling rejection, managing imposter syndrome, and keeping a positive outlook. By the end of this chapter, you'll be equipped more than Batman on a night out on the town.

Ready, Start, Job-Hunt

When you begin your journey into the job market, it's like plotting your path on a new adventure. The first crucial step is to set clear, achievable goals. Determine the types of companies that align with your aspirations and identify roles that match your skills and interests. Having these specific targets in your mind helps to narrow your focus and makes navigating the vast job landscape more manageable.

A spreadsheet can be an invaluable tool to keep your job search organized. Think of it as your job search command center. List the names of the companies, the positions you're applying for, the dates of your applications, contact persons, and any necessary follow-up actions. A living spreadsheet type of approach not only keeps you organized but also ensures you stay on top of your applications. Additionally, add brief notes to each application - little reminders of conversations or unique points about the company that could be useful in follow-ups or interviews. This level of detail helps maintain a personalized approach to each opportunity and can be a helpful reference as you progress in your job search.

Where to Look

Your job search strategy should be diverse and dynamic. Start by tapping into popular job boards like LinkedIn, Indeed, and Google Careers, which are bustling hubs of opportunity. But don't stop there. Do you remember those niche design job boards you've encountered? They can be treasure troves of specialized opportunities tailored to your field.

Expand your horizons to include Slack groups and other online design communities. These platforms can be hidden oases of job prospects, often featuring opportunities that don't make it to the larger job boards. They also provide the bonus of networking and learning from fellow professionals.

Embrace the power of AI and modern software tools to give your job hunt a competitive edge. AI can be your career matchmaker, suggesting roles that align closely with your skills and experience. Furthermore, it can be a valuable ally in tailoring your resume for specific positions. By optimizing your resume to resonate with the requirements of each job posting, you significantly boost the chances of your application catching the eye of potential employers.

Resume Building

Your resume is more than just a document; it's your first step through the door of opportunity. Keeping it updated and showcasing your current skills and experiences is essential. Employ the STAR (Situation, Task, Action, Result) method when describing your professional journey. This approach isn't just a fancy acronym; it's a way to demonstrate your impact in your roles concisely. It's a storytelling format that turns your experiences into compelling narratives of your professional growth.

Let's talk about hierarchy. If your education is your strongest suit, with little to no career experience, let it take the spotlight at the top of your resume. On the other hand, if you've dipped your toes in volunteer design work but need more formal career experience or education, highlight that volunteer experience up front. The trend here is clear: lead with your strongest cards.

Here's a potentially hot take on resumes: skip the summary. It's often just fluff and distracts from the meaty parts of your resume that recruiters are interested in. Your goal is to guide the reader's eyes to the most relevant parts of your journey, not to give them a summary of your autobiography.

Regarding length, consider your resume a Twitter post, not a blog entry – keep it to one page. Use ATS (Applicant Tracking System)-friendly templates to ensure your resume isn't lost in digital limbo. Platforms like Canva, Resume.io, and Novorésumé offer templates that strike a balance between visual appeal and ATS compatibility. And don't shy away from using AI tools for a bit of resume fine-tuning – they can help trim down your experiences to concise, impactful bullet points, ensuring each job is summarized in no more than two to three points. Remember, your resume is a highlight reel, not a director's cut.

Post Interview Tips

Following up with recruiters and interviewers is crucial. Send a thank-you email within 24 hours of your interview. You will look even better if you remember specific points about your talk. Following up shows your enthusiasm and professionalism. Be polite, express your continued interest, and reiterate how you can contribute to the role.

While career hunting, share your experience and things you have learned! Be active on platforms like LinkedIn. Share content related to design, comment on industry trends and engage with others' posts. Sharing experiences and random tidbits, you have learned keeps you visible and at the top of recruiters and hiring managers' minds when browsing the platform.

Rejection is an inevitable part of the job search. Ask for appropriate feedback, but don't be disheartened if you are ghosted. Each 'no' brings you closer to a 'yes'. Understand that rejection is not a reflection of your worth but a part of the process. Rejection may pile up, but we are in it for the long haul, remember? We discussed our goals and aren't taking our teeth out of our career goal. Keep pushing!

If you've been on the job hunt for three months with little to show, it might be time to pause and recalibrate. Reach out to mentors or tap into your network for advice. These people can be like your career GPS, helping you navigate uncertain territories.

For example, getting to the interview stage but not sealing the deal with an offer is a signal to polish your interview skills. Think of interviews like auditions – every performance needs rehearsal and fine-tuning. There are numerous resources, from online workshops to practice interviews, that can help you improve your technique. A second example, you're not even getting interviews. That may be a sign to work on your resume or review your portfolio. Think about what people see first when you're applying. We recommend using the same resume for at least a month before changing it. Constantly updating it repeatedly doesn't return trustworthy metrics, making it hard to know what works.

As for tackling imposter syndrome, it's about giving yourself credit where it's due—feeling unsure sometimes. Take a moment to reflect on your journey – your skills, experiences, and the unique flavors you bring to the design table. Each of these is a badge of your professional journey, a reminder that you've earned your place in the field. Remember, even the most seasoned professionals have moments of doubt; what sets them apart is their ability to acknowledge these feelings and proceed with confidence. You're a step further than you were when you started this book. It's hard to forget our tiny steps on a long journey.

Job hunting is a journey filled with ups and downs. Stay organized, leverage your network, and use the tools. Remember to stay positive and persistent. Each step is a learning experience that brings you closer to your goal.

Up next, we'll prepare for the long haul in your journey. We'll discuss strategies for sustaining momentum, continuing to learn and grow, and preparing for the ever-evolving landscape of the design industry.

THE LONG HAUL

Embarking on a career in design is not a sprint; it's a marathon. This chapter is dedicated to the long-term strategies and mindsets that will sustain you through the ups and downs of a design career. We'll talk about continuous learning, networking, setting realistic goals and timelines, managing expectations, and the importance of self-care. This journey is about persistence, adaptability, and maintaining your passion for design, even when the road gets tough.

Staying Current

In the fast-paced world of design, staying current is critical. Keep up with the latest trends and mainstream applications. Regularly review popular apps and websites, and practice incorporating their design elements into your work. Staying up to date keeps your skills sharp and helps you understand current user expectations and preferences, which is crucial for making informed design decisions in your job. Use websites like Mobbin.design to review wireframes from companies and memorize what the industry is doing. If it helps, spend some time each week doing design challenges to keep your skills brushed up. We want to get to a place where we are so busy with paid work that we don't need to do this, but it's always imperative to play with apps and keep tabs on what the world is designing!

Yes, keep networking! It probably gets old hearing that throughout this book, but everyone says this is the puzzle's most crucial piece. Building and maintaining a professional network is essential, no matter where you are in your career. New mentors can provide fresh perspectives and guidance, helping you navigate challenges and seize opportunities. Remind yourself to keep in contact with people you meet that are important to keep in your circle. Be friendly and stay at the top of your mind; it's as simple as that.

Don't hesitate to reach out to people whose work you admire or hold positions you aspire to. Networking isn't just about advancing your career; it's about building a community of like-minded professionals who can support and inspire each other.

Goals and Expectations

As you navigate the job market, remember those goals and timelines you initially etched out. They're your roadmap. Stick to them, but be flexible enough to take detours as needed. The design industry is ever-changing, so regular reviews and tweaks to your strategy are as essential as software updates on your favorite design tool.

UX design is all about strategy, which should also extend to your career development. Be as methodical and deliberate in planning your career moves as you would be in crafting a user experience. If something isn't clicking, don't be afraid to pivot. Regular self-check-ins are crucial – like your career's periodic health check-ups, ensuring you stay on track toward your long-term aspirations.

There's no shame in asking for help. So, set realistic expectations, especially in a job market as competitive as design. Starting can be challenging, and success rarely happens overnight. Whether for project advice, feedback, or career guidance, remember that reaching out is a sign of strength and resourcefulness. Everyone starts somewhere, and the design community is generally a supportive bunch, ready to lend a hand or an ear.

If persistence and asking for health are getting you to a breaking point, remember even the best designers need to hit the pause button. Design can be demanding, so balancing work with rest and personal interests is crucial. Regular breaks aren't just good for your well-being and keep your creative energies flowing. It may sometimes be easy to get sucked into the endless funnel and not wanting to quit until your end goal, but we all don't know when that will be. While managing stress is essential, remember that financial and time management are key. It's wise to have backup plans, like part-time gigs or freelancing. Be prepared to adapt your strategies to sustain your career without running your reserves dry. We have seen people run themselves into a corner by not planning or being realistic, so we give you these reminders. What are friends for, right?

Landing your first paid gig is just the beginning. Keep nurturing your portfolio, stay engaged with your network, and constantly seek out new challenges. Proactively building your skills and experience is critical to long-term success. When you're in your paid gig, make sure to be thinking about what you want to learn from your current place of work. It could be a specific subject. It could be as simple as soaking up all the knowledge of the senior designers you're working with.

Most importantly, remember to have fun and pursue what excites you! Early career jobs might not be dream gigs, but they're stepping stones. Keep your passion for design at the forefront, and rewarding opportunities will eventually come your way.

As we wrap up this chapter, it's essential to remember that your design career is a journey, complete with its own set of highs and lows. Like a rollercoaster, it's thrilling, unpredictable, and sometimes scary, but always moving forward. Our next chapter will dive into the nitty-gritty of keeping your momentum going. We'll explore practical strategies for overcoming the inevitable challenges and capitalizing on the opportunities that come your way in this dynamic field.

Remember, persistence and passion are your compass and map in this journey. They will guide you through the twists and turns, helping you navigate toward success in the vibrant and constantly evolving design world.

WRAPPING UP

As we conclude this guide, let's reflect on our journey together. This handbook empowers aspiring designers, offering insights and strategies for carving a successful UX, UI, and product design path. Let's recap the essential themes and lessons that have been the backbone of this adventure.

We started by challenging the notion that formal education is the sole route to success in design. This book hits the idea that passion, dedication, and a growth mindset are equally crucial. It's a beacon for self-taught individuals, career switchers, and design explorers, illuminating the myriad paths available in this field.

We dove into the intricacies of UX, UI, and product design, shedding light on their unique aspects, necessary skills, and potential career trajectories. This deep dive was designed to help you pinpoint and pursue your niche with clarity and confidence.

A significant emphasis was placed on visualizing your desired role in design and establishing tangible career objectives. We discussed the significance of contemplating different work environments and aspiring for higher echelons in design. The guide underscored the importance of setting timelines and tracking your progress as crucial ingredients for success.

The themes of perpetual learning and networking recur throughout this book. We hope you are sick of hearing some of these words, but we did it to make you invincible. In the ever-changing design world, staying updated and connected is not just recommended; it's essential. Networking, both within your immediate sphere and beyond, was spotlighted as crucial for professional development and uncovering new opportunities.

We delved into the criticality of crafting a personal brand and a compelling portfolio. Your brand is your distinct professional identity, while your portfolio is a living document of your skills and experiences. Together, they are indispensable tools for showcasing talent and standing out in a competitive landscape. The key word is "living document," which means constantly updating it as you grow.

The book offered hands-on advice for acquiring volunteer experience, presenting your designs, and tackling the job market. It equipped you with tactics for gaining practical experience, handling feedback constructively, and navigating job hunting efficiently. We covered everything from crafting an impactful resume to acing interviews and leveraging social media for professional growth.

The journey in design is long and filled with both challenges and victories. We touched on the importance of resilience, adaptability, and sustaining your passion and creativity. Recognizing market realities, setting realistic expectations, and preparing for ongoing growth and learning are vital for a fulfilling design career.

As this handbook concludes, remember that your path as a designer is unique and ever-changing. The insights and advice provided here are not just stepping stones but guiding lights as your runways take off! Keep the flame of learning alive, stay inquisitive, and embrace your journey with zeal and resolve.

Please reach out if you need more in-depth advice, help, or support. The QR code below will take you to my LinkedIn profile. Follow me, and feel free to check out some of the things I post as they relate to some of the things we've covered here!

In case you missed it, here is a link to my resources list!
danadarr.info

REFERENCES

2023 Product Designer salary in US | Built in. (n.d.). https://builtin.com/salaries/product/product-designer

2023 UI Designer salary in US | Built in. (n.d.). https://builtin.com/salaries/design-ux/ui-designer

2023 UX Designer salary in US | Built in. (n.d.). https://builtin.com/salaries/design-ux/ux-designer

Product Designer salary in 2023 | PayScale. (n.d.). https://www.payscale.com/research/US/Job=Product_Designer/Salary

Salary.com. (n.d.-a). *Product Designer Salary | Salary.com.* https://www.salary.com/research/salary/listing/product-designer-salary

Salary.com. (n.d.-b). *User Interface Designer Salary | Salary.com.* https://www.salary.com/research/salary/listing/user-interface-designer-salary

Salary.com. (n.d.-c). *UX Designer Salary | Salary.com.* https://www.salary.com/research/salary/listing/ux-designer-salary

User Interface Designer salary in 2023 | PayScale. (n.d.-a). https://www.payscale.com/research/US/Job=User_Interface_Designer/Salary

User Interface Designer salary in 2023 | PayScale. (n.d.-b). https://www.payscale.com/research/US/Job=User_Interface_Designer/Salary

UX Designer salary in 2023 | PayScale. (n.d.). https://www.payscale.com/research/US/Job=UX_Designer/Salary

www.ingramcontent.com/pod-product-compliance
Lightning Source LLC
LaVergne TN
LVHW051749050326
832903LV00029B/2819

* 9 7 9 8 8 8 4 6 3 7 9 1 7 *